SHOOTING GUARD

By Jason Glaser

Gareth Stevens
Publishing

Please visit our Web site, www.garethstevens.com. For a free color catalog of all our high-quality books, call toll free 1-800-542-2595 or fax 1-877-542-2596.

Library of Congress Cataloging-in-Publication Data

Glaser, Jason.
Shooting guard / Jason Glaser.
    p. cm. — (Tip-off, basketball)
Includes index.
ISBN 978-1-4339-3981-5 (pbk.)
ISBN 978-1-4339-3982-2 (6 pack)
ISBN 978-1-4339-3980-8 (library binding)
1. Guards (Basketball) I. Title.
GV885.G56 2011
796.323—dc22

                                        2010012451

First Edition

Published in 2011 by
Gareth Stevens Publishing
111 East 14th Street, Suite 349
New York, NY 10003

Designer: Haley W. Harasymiw
Editor: Greg Roza

Gareth Stevens Publishing would like to thank consultant Stephen Hayn, men's basketball coach at Dowling College, for his guidance in writing this book.

Photo credits: Cover, p. 1 (Kobe Bryant) Evan Goal/Getty Images; cover, back cover, pp. 2, 3, 5, 7, 11, 17, 41, 44–48 (basketball court background on all), 7, 8, 12, 14, 20, 22, 38, 42, 43 (basketball border on all), 40 Shutterstock.com; p. 4 Robert Sullivan/AFP/Getty Images; p. 5 Scott Winterton/NBAE via Getty Images; pp. 6, 7 Hulton Archive/Getty Images; p. 8 Orlando/Three Lions/Getty Images; pp. 10, 12 Focus on Sports/Getty Images; p. 11 Dick Raphael/NBAE via Getty Images; p. 13 Don Grayston/NBAE via Getty Images; pp. 14, 32 Nathaniel S. Butler/NBAE/Getty Images; p. 15 © Manny Milan/Sports Illutrated/Getty Images; p. 17 Ronald Martinez/Getty Images; p. 18 Noah Graham/NBAE via Getty Images; pp. 19, 24 Christian Petersen/Getty Images; pp. 20, 27 Glenn James/NBAE via Getty Images; p. 21 Nick Laham/Getty Images; p. 22 Joe Murphy/NBAE via Getty Images; pp. 23, 38 Kevin C. Cox/Getty Images; pp. 25, 30 Fernando Medina/NBAE via Getty Images; pp. 26, 37 Jonathan Daniel/Getty Images; p. 29 Chris Graythen/Getty Images; pp. 31, 35 Jed Jacobsohn/ Getty Images; p. 33 © Ned Dishman; pp. 34, 44 Stephen Dunn/Getty Images; pp. 36, 39 Elsa/Getty Images; pp. 41, 42, 43 © iStockphoto.com.

Printed in the United States of America

CPSIA compliance information: Batch #CS10GS: For further information contact Gareth Stevens, New York, New York at 1-800-542-2595.

CONTENTS

Boldface words appear in the glossary.

The Game Winners

In basketball, as in most sports, whoever gets the most points wins. Teams need shooters who can make baskets from anywhere on the court. With the game on the line, the ball goes to the shooting guard.

Going Out on Top

There's no bigger name in basketball than former shooting guard Michael Jordan. On June 14, 1998, Jordan and the Chicago Bulls were playing for a sixth **NBA** championship. With just over 40 seconds left in the game, the Bulls trailed the Utah Jazz by 3 points. The Bulls got the ball to Jordan, who **dribbled** around defenders and made a basket.

After winning three straight championships with the Bulls, Jordan retired in 1993. However, he returned to the Bulls in 1995 and led them to three more championships!

4

The Jazz were ahead by one point. They tried to run down the clock. Determined to win, Jordan snuck around the Jazz's Karl Malone, stole the ball, and headed for the basket. After making a fake move that caused Jazz player Byron Russell to fall down, Jordan took a wide-open shot that swished through the net. The Bulls won the game and the championship! The NBA later judged Jordan's performance to be the greatest moment in finals history.

Jordan fakes out Byron Russell on his way to the basket in the last game of the 1998 NBA Finals.

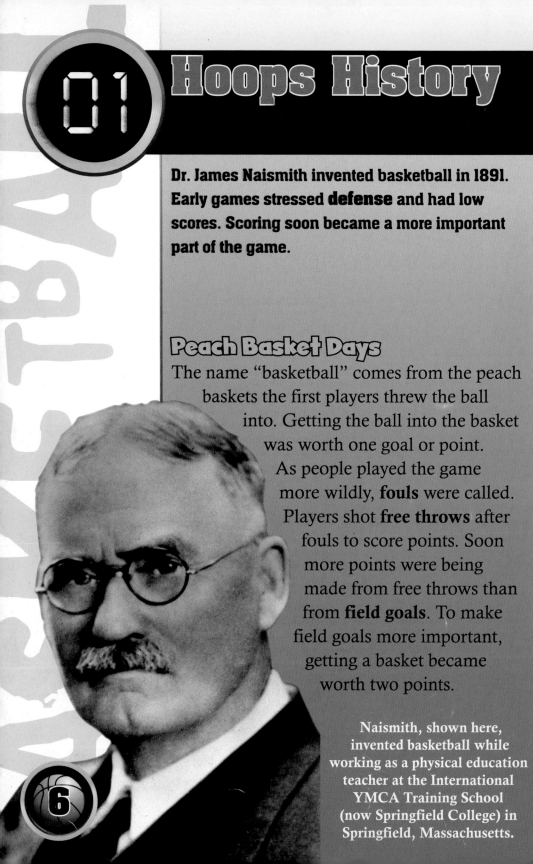

Dr. James Naismith invented basketball in 1891. Early games stressed **defense** and had low scores. Scoring soon became a more important part of the game.

Peach Basket Days

The name "basketball" comes from the peach baskets the first players threw the ball into. Getting the ball into the basket was worth one goal or point. As people played the game more wildly, **fouls** were called. Players shot **free throws** after fouls to score points. Soon more points were being made from free throws than from **field goals**. To make field goals more important, getting a basket became worth two points.

Naismith, shown here, invented basketball while working as a physical education teacher at the International YMCA Training School (now Springfield College) in Springfield, Massachusetts.

Dribblers and Shooters

At first, officials felt that dribbling the ball made it too easy to make baskets. They made a rule that said dribblers couldn't shoot the ball. To get points, dribbling players needed to pass the ball to a teammate who could take a shot. Teams worked to get good shooters open while players with ball-handling skills controlled the ball.

This is a picture of Naismith (center row, left) and his first basketball team.

From Defense to Offense

Originally, a guard's job was simply to keep the other team from scoring. Guards stayed near the **opponent's** basket. When the other team had the ball, the guards defended the basket. On **offense**, guards who wanted to take a shot at their own basket often had to shoot from far away.

A shooting guard takes a shot from 20 feet out during a game in 1948.

Some basketball leagues wanted to reward players who became good at shooting from farther away. During the 1960s, one of the professional leagues added a half circle at each end of the court. Shots made from outside the line were worth three points. Good long-distance shooters could put up much higher point totals. By the 1980s, the three-point shot was allowed at all levels of play.

three-point line

Official Distances for the Three-Point Line

U.S. High School and College (women): 19 feet 9 inches (6.02 m)

U.S. College (men): 20 feet 9 inches (6.32 m)

WNBA: 20 feet 6 inches (6.25 m)

Major International Competition (beginning 2010) and World (beginning 2012): 22 feet 2 inches (6.75 m)

NBA: 22 feet (6.71 m) at sidelines, 23 feet 9 inches (7.24 m) at center

There have been many great shooting guards in NBA history. Here are a few of the finest to play the game.

Ten-Time Champion

In Sam Jones's 12 years with the Boston Celtics, the team won 10 NBA championships. From 1957 to 1969, Jones used his highly practiced **bank shot** to get over 15,000 points and become one of the league's top scorers. Many basketball fans believe Jones had one of the best jump shots of all time.

In 1996, Jones was selected as one of the 50 Greatest Players in NBA History.

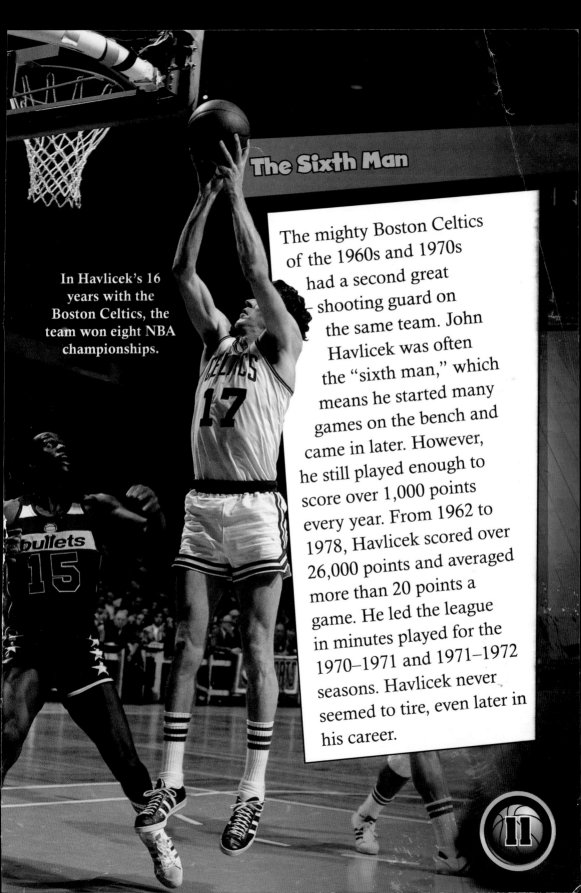

In Havlicek's 16 years with the Boston Celtics, the team won eight NBA championships.

The mighty Boston Celtics of the 1960s and 1970s had a second great shooting guard on the same team. John Havlicek was often the "sixth man," which means he started many games on the bench and came in later. However, he still played enough to score over 1,000 points every year. From 1962 to 1978, Havlicek scored over 26,000 points and averaged more than 20 points a game. He led the league in minutes played for the 1970–1971 and 1971–1972 seasons. Havlicek never seemed to tire, even later in his career.

On the West Side

Dave Bing

The Los Angeles Lakers' Jerry West netted over 25,000 points in 14 seasons and won the championship in 1972. He was an All-Star every year he played. West gave everything he had. In the 1969 finals, he played while injured and was named Finals **MVP**. No other player has ever won the award while playing for the losing team.

Vision of Greatness

Many who watched Dave Bing play had better eyesight than he did. Bing had hurt his left eye as a boy, but he still learned to shoot baskets. He played from 1966 to 1978, mostly with the Detroit Pistons. For the 1967–1968 season, he led the league in scoring. Bing was a smart player who became a smart businessman. He started a steel company in Detroit and was elected mayor of the city in 2009.

Drexler played for the Portland Trail Blazers from 1983 to 1995. In 1995, he was traded to the Houston Rockets. He helped the Rockets win the NBA Championship that year.

The Swingman

Clyde Drexler was a rare shooting guard who disliked scoring from far away. Instead, he used his size to **dunk**. Drexler became a model for big guards who played like forwards. A shooting guard who plays near the basket like Drexler is called a "swingman."

No one benefited more from the three-point line than Reggie Miller. Miller won countless close games for the Indiana Pacers with fourth-quarter heroics and last-second three-point shots. In one playoff game, Miller scored eight points in 8.9 seconds. Miller made 2,560 three-pointers in his 18 years with the Pacers, more than anyone else in NBA history.

Miller makes a three-point shot in a game against the Detroit Pistons in 1988.

Jordan earned the nickname "Air Jordan" because of his dazzling leaps from the free-throw line when dunking.

Air Jordan

To many, Michael Jordan was the greatest basketball player of all time. He led the league in scoring for 11 of his 15 seasons, including 7 years in a row from 1986 to 1993. He averaged over 30 points per game for his entire career. He won six championships and six Finals MVP awards, as well as five league MVP awards. He could shoot from a distance or fly through the air and dunk over defenders. He was equally dangerous on defense, leading the league in steals three times.

15

03 Playing as a Shooting Guard

Being a shooting guard involves more than throwing the ball at the basket. Shooting guards have to work hard just to make a shot. Here are the keys to putting up points.

Getting in Position

As the offense sets up, the shooting guard starts in the back court and off to one side. Many times, the point guard signals who will be getting the ball or taking the shot. This lets the shooting guard know where to be.

By starting in the back court, the shooting guard is in position to take a three-point shot if he's open.

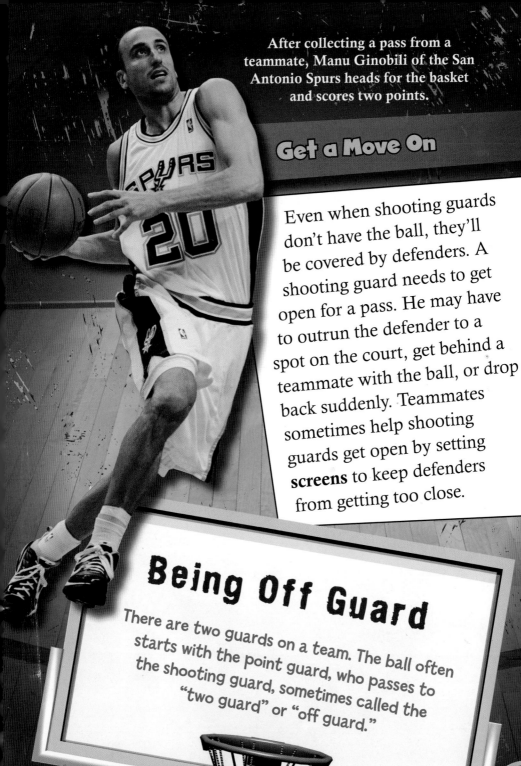

After collecting a pass from a teammate, Manu Ginobili of the San Antonio Spurs heads for the basket and scores two points.

Get a Move On

Even when shooting guards don't have the ball, they'll be covered by defenders. A shooting guard needs to get open for a pass. He may have to outrun the defender to a spot on the court, get behind a teammate with the ball, or drop back suddenly. Teammates sometimes help shooting guards get open by setting **screens** to keep defenders from getting too close.

Being Off Guard

There are two guards on a team. The ball often starts with the point guard, who passes to the shooting guard, sometimes called the "two guard" or "off guard."

Getting Open

There are many ways a shooting guard can get free long enough to catch a pass. The most common way is by using cuts.

Front and Back Cuts

The simplest cut is a quick run past a defender. In a front cut, the shooting guard darts in front of a defender to reach the basket. In a back cut, the shooting guard passes behind the defender before reaching the basket. In both cases, a well-timed pass can reach the shooting guard while he's closer to the basket than the defender.

Mike Dunleavy of the Indiana Pacers makes a back cut around an opponent to get close to the basket.

The V Cut

An easy way to escape a defender is to trick the opponent into going somewhere else. If a shooting guard takes a few steps in one direction, the defender might follow him. The guard can then run back the other way while the defender's still moving in the other direction. This is called a V cut because the shooting guard's movements trace a V shape on the floor.

Sacramento King Kevin Martin gets open for a jump shot after making a V cut.

When the opponent uses a man-to-man defense, each defender follows one offensive player closely. Curl cuts can break up the defense and cause confusion. The shooting guard circles around a teammate. In order to stay close to the shooting guard, the defender has to get past the guard's teammate as well as the player defending the teammate. The guard's teammate may also set up a screen. This can cause the defense to bunch up, allowing the shooting guard to get open to take a shot.

Jason Terry of the Dallas Mavericks curls around teammate Dirk Nowitzki.

The L Cut

For the L cut, the shooting guard runs hard in one direction, usually at the basket. The guard then turns quickly to one side and moves into the pass. His path should look like an L. If done right, the defender won't be able to stop and turn fast enough to break up the pass. The shooting guard then turns away to get open and avoid running into the defender.

A well-timed L cut can allow a shooting guard, like Raja Bell of the Charlotte Hornets, to get open for a jump shot.

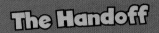

The Handoff

In some cases, the shooting guard and point guard run at each other. With no one between them, the guards can hand the ball off as they pass. The shooting guard can turn and shoot while the point guard screens the defense. If the defense moves in on the shooting guard during the handoff, the shooting guard can screen for the point guard instead.

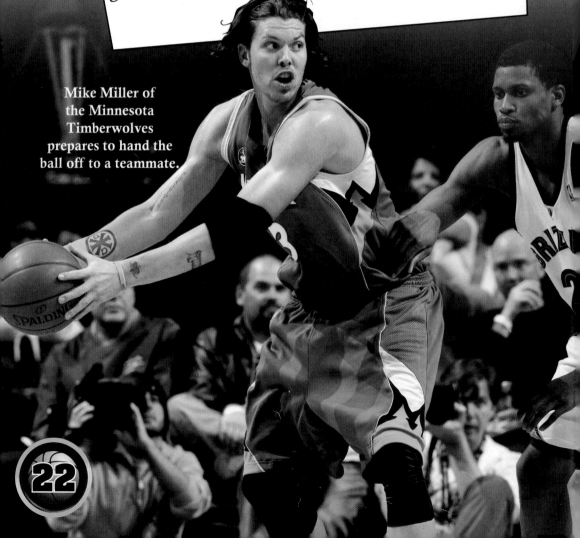

Mike Miller of the Minnesota Timberwolves prepares to hand the ball off to a teammate.

If a shooting guard is good at getting open, the defense might **double-team** him. By making a sudden cut, the shooting guard can draw two or three defenders away from their positions. This is called a leading cut because the guard leads the defenders away from the action. His teammates are then open to score or pass to someone else.

A quick-thinking shooting guard like Joe Johnson of the Atlanta Hawks can help teammates get open by performing a leading cut.

23

Key Skills

A player can't score without good **fundamentals**. Here's what every shooting guard needs to know.

Playing Catch

Before the shooting guard can make a basket, he needs the ball. When a pass comes, he needs to catch it cleanly, protect the ball, and shoot quickly. Shooting guards must move toward the ball in flight. This makes it less likely that the pass will be caught by a defender. The shooting guard draws the ball in and comes to a quick stop. He's now ready to act.

Once Jason Richardson of the Phoenix Suns catches the ball, he's ready to make a play.

If the shooting guard moves more than one foot, he needs to be dribbling or he'll be called for **traveling**. If a player stops dribbling, he can't start again or move. To turn around without traveling, a player pivots—he keeps one foot firmly on the ground and spins on it. With a quick pivot, a shooting guard can twist around and shoot or pass cleanly to a teammate.

Jamal Crawford of the Atlanta Hawks pivots on one foot while looking at the basket.

For a clean shot, the shooting guard needs to be able to beat his defender one-on-one. He may have to drive in toward the basket and protect the ball with his body. He might have to fake a shot or a drive to get a defender off balance before moving. Or he may try to outrun a defender on a fast break. Finding a way to get by a defender is the key to making a lot of baskets.

Brandon Roy of the Portland Trail Balzers beats a defender one-on-one.

Foul Is Fair

One way to get points is through fouls. If you have good one-on-one skills, a defender may commit a foul to stop you. This lets you take free throws!

The Jumper

Getting the ball to the basket isn't easy when tall people wave their long arms in your face. A shooting guard needs to get the ball up and over big defenders when he shoots. By jumping into the air before shooting, a shooting guard can get the extra height he needs to **arc** the ball to the basket. A good jump shooter has to be **accurate** even while up in the air!

Considered by many to be the best player in the NBA, Kobe Bryant of the Los Angeles Lakers has an amazingly accurate jump shot.

The Sweet Spot

Good shooting guards need to feel comfortable scoring from a number of different spots on the court. Most guards have favorite places to shoot from. They practice shots from these spots most often. But they need to practice shots from all over the court, too.

Point and Shoot

The point is the spot at the top of the three-point line, directly in front of the basket. Making a shot from there is like making a long free throw. A shooting guard can drop the shot through the hoop or use the backboard to bring the ball down through the rim. The orange rectangle on the backboard works like a target for the shooter.

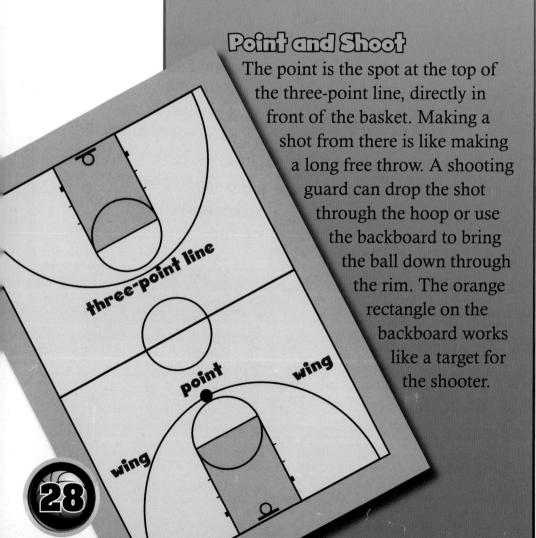

three-point line

point

wing

wing

The area outside the three-point line between the point and the corner is called the wing. From here, the shooting guard is at a 45-degree angle to the basket. The shooter still has a chance to bank the ball off the backboard if he needs to. A missed shot from the wing can **rebound** in any direction, so a guard shooting from the wing needs to make an accurate shot.

Kevin Durant shoots for three points from the wing.

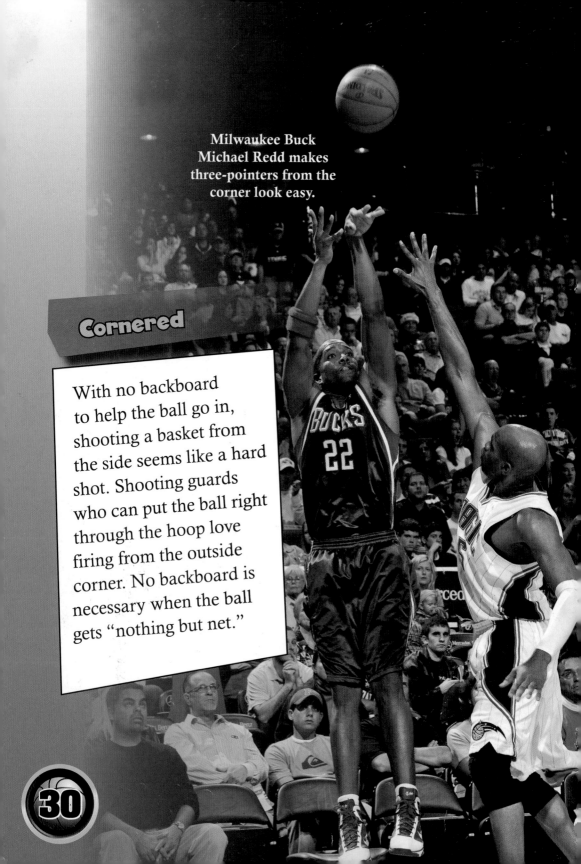

Milwaukee Buck Michael Redd makes three-pointers from the corner look easy.

Cornered

With no backboard to help the ball go in, shooting a basket from the side seems like a hard shot. Shooting guards who can put the ball right through the hoop love firing from the outside corner. No backboard is necessary when the ball gets "nothing but net."

Post Haste

The post lines that run between the free-throw line and the **baseline** help form the area called the free-throw lane, or post. No player on offense can be in this area for more than 3 seconds unless a shot is taken. If he can get into this lane, a shooter can get a closer shot. From the low post near the basket, a shooter can bank a shot off the backboard. From the high post, a player can make a close jump shot.

Dwyane Wade of the Miami Heat—shown here during the 2010 NBA All-Star Game—is a master with the ball from the low post.

The Playbook

To play well, teams must practice well. Teams think up dozens of ways to get the shooting guard open, and the shooting guard must know them all.

Learn the Defense

Many types of defense exist. A team might cover each player man-to-man or make each defender responsible for a single area using **zone defense**. The coach makes the team practice against the style of defense used by their next opponent. The shooting guard practices plays that give him the best chance of being open or getting to the basket against that type of defense.

An excellent defender for the New York Knicks, Larry Hughes helps his team keep the lead against the Philadelphia 76ers.

In basketball, everyone plays both offense and defense. Good shooting guards learn to cut off passes, steal balls, and defend shots. Learning defense helps with playing offense. The better a shooter can think like a defender, the better he will be at beating defenders in a game.

Ray Allen of the Boston Celtics keeps the opponent from scoring on a fast break.

The Guard Part of Shooting Guard

As an outside player, a shooting guard may be all that stands between the other team and an easy basket on a **turnover**. If the opponent takes the ball the other way, a shooting guard's job is to contain the ball handler until his team can set up on defense.

Some of pro basketball's greatest superstars are playing in the NBA right now. Let's take a look at today's top shooting guards.

The Young Gun

On January 21, 2010, Kobe Bryant became the youngest player to reach 25,000 points. The 31-year-old Los Angeles Laker is the sixteenth-leading scorer of all-time and perhaps the best player in the game today. On January 22, 2006, he scored 81 points in one game. He's helped the Lakers win four championships, including three in a row from 2000 to 2002—when it seemed no one could beat Bryant or the Lakers.

In 2008, Bryant helped the U.S. Men's Basketball Team win a gold medal at the Summer Olympics in Beijing, China.

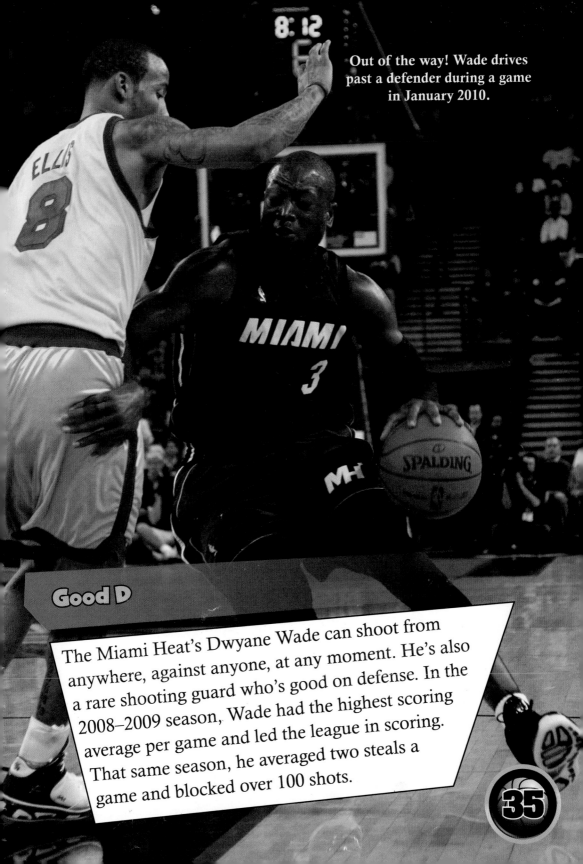

Out of the way! Wade drives past a defender during a game in January 2010.

Good D

The Miami Heat's Dwyane Wade can shoot from anywhere, against anyone, at any moment. He's also a rare shooting guard who's good on defense. In the 2008–2009 season, Wade had the highest scoring average per game and led the league in scoring. That same season, he averaged two steals a game and blocked over 100 shots.

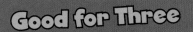

Playing for the Boston
Celtics, Ray Allen
wears the number
20. It might be
more fitting
if he wore
number 3. Allen
has the record for
most three-pointers
in a season. He also
has the record for most
three-pointers in the NBA
Finals. He once made eight
three-pointers in the second
half of a game, tying another
record. Allen is currently
second to Reggie Miller in
career three-pointers.

Allen made 22 three-point
shots during the 2008 NBA
Finals against the Los
Angeles Lakers. This broke
the previous record of 17.

The Natural

When Brandon Roy joined the Portland Trail Blazers, he had to take over scoring and leadership roles right away. He began the 2006–2007 season as a **rookie**, and by the end he'd been named Rookie of the Year. His scoring average, impressive play, and game-winning shots made him the favorite for 127 out of 128 judges. In 2009, Roy led the Trail Blazers back to the playoffs for the first time since 2003.

Brandon Roy (center) of the Portland Trail Blazers looks to pass under pressure from Loul Deng (left) and Derrick Rose (right) of the Chicago Bulls.

The Ironman

Some players can really play the game of basketball. Joe Johnson of the Atlanta Hawks is known to play the whole game, every game! In the 2003–2004 season, Johnson led the league in minutes played. All those minutes don't tire his shooting arm. Over his career, Johnson has made 44.2 percent of his shots. One year, he made almost half of his 370 three-point shots.

Joe Johnson

Help for Haiti

In January 2010, a huge earthquake struck the country of Haiti. After that disaster, Joe Johnson and other NBA players promised that for one game they would donate $1,000 to Haiti for every point they made. Johnson scored 19 points!

38

During the 2003–2004 season, Richard "Rip" Hamilton had his nose broken so badly he needed a mask to protect it. That year, Hamilton's points and **assists** guided the Detroit Pistons to a championship. Hamilton has continued to wear the mask each season. Hamilton has scored over 1,200 points every year since the 2000–2001 season. He's helped lead the Pistons to the playoffs every year since joining the team in 2002. Inspired by Hamilton, college and high school players with face injuries often wear "Rip masks" rather than risk further injury.

During the 2008 playoffs, Hamilton became the Pistons' all-time leader in postseason points.

39

05 Future Star: You!

Hoping to shoot with the pros some day? Here are some things you'll need to work on.

The Quick Shot

Shooting guards may only have a moment to shoot after receiving a pass. Have some friends give you some quick passes one after another. Shoot the ball right after getting each pass. Once you've got this down, face away from the basket to receive the passes. You'll need to pivot toward the basket before shooting. Try to be able to turn from any direction and still score consistently.

This player holds the ball firmly as he pivots to make a shot.

Warning!

Stopping or changing direction suddenly can injure your muscles and joints if not done properly. Never lock your knees. Bend low and wide through the legs. Use your hips and thighs for power.

The Pull-Up Jumper

Coming to a hard stop from a run in order to shoot a basket is tricky. Practice dribbling quickly toward the basket from midcourt. When you're about 15 feet away, stop and take a jump shot. Your body should go straight up, not forward. Power your jump with your legs and hips, and shoot from the highest point in your jump. This shot is called the pull-up jumper.

The jump shot is an important part of a shooting guard's game. Practice from many different areas of the court.

41

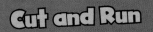

Place a chair somewhere in the wing area on one side of the basket. Pretend the chair is a defender. Have a teammate ready with the ball outside the three-point line. Run at the chair. As you reach it, stop and pivot to the inside. Your friend should pass the ball to you as you turn. Catch the ball and take it to the basket for a **layup**.

Once you've perfected this drill with a chair, ask a friend to be the defender.

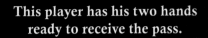

This player has his two hands ready to receive the pass.

Pass Catching

Players move into a pass to keep it from being caught by the other team. Take a step or two toward a friend as he passes to you. Keep your eyes on the ball and bring it in with two hands. Your hands and arms should be relaxed just enough so the ball doesn't bounce off accidentally. Make sure you come to a complete stop as soon as you catch the ball so you don't travel. For a challenge, run toward your partner as he passes to practice catching on the move.

Record Book

What shooting guards have made the most baskets? Take a look at these numbers.

Career Points by a Shooting Guard:

1. Michael Jordan	32,292
2. George Gervin	26,595
3. John Havlicek	26,395
4. Kobe Bryant (still active)	25,486 (as of 3/4/10)
5. Reggie Miller	25,279

Kobe Bryant

Single-Season Points by a Shooting Guard:

1. Michael Jordan	3,041	1986–1987
2. Michael Jordan	2,868	1987–1988
3. Kobe Bryant (still active)	2,832	2005–2006
4. Michael Jordan	2,753	1989–1990
5. Michael Jordan	2,633	1988–1989

Points in a Game by a Shooting Guard:

1. Kobe Bryant (still active)	81	1/22/06
2. David Thompson	73	4/9/78
3. Michael Jordan	69	3/28/90
4. Kobe Bryant (still active)	65	3/16/07
5. Michael Jordan	64	1/16/93

Career Three-Pointers by a Shooting Guard

1. Reggie Miller	**2,560**
2. Ray Allen (still active)	**2,444** (as of 5/20/10)
3. Dale Ellis	**1,719**
4. Glen Rice	**1,559**
5. Eddie Jones	**1,546**

Three-Pointers in a Season by a Shooting Guard:

1. Ray Allen (still active)	**269**	2005–2006
2. Jason Richardson (still active)	**243**	2007–2008
3. Reggie Miller	**229**	1996–1997
4. Ray Allen (still active)	**229**	2001–2002
5. Quentin Richardson (still active)	**226**	2007–2008

Three-Pointers in a Single Game by a Shooting Guard:

1. Kobe Bryant (still active)	12	1/7/03
2. J. R. Smith (still active)	11	4/13/09
3. J. R. Smith (still active)	10	12/23/09
Ray Allen (still active)	10	4/14/02
Joe Dumars	10	11/08/94

All-Star Game Appearances by a Shooting Guard:

1. Michael Jordan	14
Jerry West	14
3. John Havlicek	13
4. Kobe Bryant (still active)	12
5. Clyde Drexler	10

45

Glossary

accurate: exact and free from errors

arc: to shoot a ball on a high, curved path instead of a straight one

assist: when a player makes a pass that enables a teammate to score

bank shot: a basket made by bouncing the ball off the backboard and then into the hoop

baseline: the line behind the basket that marks the end of the court

defense: the act of trying to stop the other team from scoring

double-team: when two people defend against a single player

dribble: to move around the court while bouncing the ball

dunk: to throw the basketball into the basket from above the rim

field goal: a basket made during normal play

foul: a penalty called for breaking rules, usually coming from illegal contact between players

free throw: a chance to shoot for one point afterr being fouled; the shot is made from a line in front of the basket with no defenders

fundamentals: basic skills

layup: a shot made from beneath the basket by bouncing the ball off the backboard and into the net

MVP: most valuable player

NBA: National Basketball Association, the men's professional basketball league in the United States; the NBA also includes the Toronto (Canada) Raptors

offense: the team trying to score

opponent: the person or team you must beat to win a game

rebound: bounce off the rim

rookie: a player in his first year playing a sport

screen: a play where a player moves to block a defender to give a teammate a chance to get open for a pass

travel: to take two or more steps with the ball before passing, shooting, or dribbling

turnover: when a team loses control of the ball to the opponent

WNBA: Women's National Basketball Association, the women's professional basketball league in the United States

zone defense: a playing style in which defenders are responsible for guarding any opposing players who enter their area of the court

For More Information

Books

Bowen, Fred. *The Final Cut*. Atlanta, GA: Peachtree Publishers, 2009.

Christopher, Matt. *Center Court Sting*. Chicago, IL: Little Brown Books, 2007.

Doeden, Matt. *The World's Greatest Basketball Players*. Mankato, MN: Capstone Press, 2010.

Eule, Brian. *Basketball for Fun!* Minneapolis, MN: Compass Point Books, 2003.

Lupica, Mike. *Hot Hand*. Boston, MA: Walden Media, 2007.

Schaller, Bob, and Coach Dave Harnish. *The Everything Kids' Basketball Book*. Avon, MA: Adams Media, 2009.

Wallace, Rich. *Dunk Under Pressure*. New York, NY: Viking Books, 2006.

Web Sites

www.hoophall.com
Learn the history of basketball at the online version of the Naismith Memorial Basketball Hall of Fame. Read biographies of the greatest basketball players of all time.

www.nba.com
The official Web site of the National Basketball Association has information about teams and players both current and historic. Fans can see video, get news, check scores, and look over game or season statistics.

www.nba.com/kids
The NBA's official Web site for kids that lets you play games, join fan clubs for your favorite team, and learn exercises to make you a better basketball player.

www.sikids.com/basketball/nba
The *Sports Illustrated* site for kids lets you follow your favorite NBA team. On this site, you'll find scores and news updates about your favorite sport.

Index

About the Author

Jason Glaser is a freelance writer and stay-at-home father living in Mankato, Minnesota. He has written over fifty nonfiction books for children, including books on sports stars such as Tim Duncan. When he isn't listening to sports radio or writing, Jason likes to play volleyball and put idealized versions of himself into sports video games.

CC

Central Childrens

NOV

2010